Abigail Adams

History Maker Bios

Jane Sutcliffe

LERNER PUBLICATIONS COMPANY • MINNEAPOLIS

J
BIO
ADAMS

Lerner Publications Company
A division of Lerner Publishing Group
241 First Avenue North
Minneapolis, MN 55401 U.S.A.

Website address: www.lernerbooks.com

Library of Congress Cataloging-in-Publication Data

Sutcliffe, Jane.
    Abigail Adams / by Jane Sutcliffe.
       p.   cm. — (History maker bios)
    Includes bibliographical references and index.
    ISBN-13: 978-0-8225-5942-9 (lib. bdg. : alk. paper)
    ISBN-10: 0-8225-5942-0 (lib. bdg. : alk. paper)
    1. Adams, Abigail, 1744–1818—Juvenile literature. 2. Presidents' spouses—United States—Biography—Juvenile literature. I. Title. II. Series.
    E322.1.A38S88 2006
    973.4'4092—dc22   2005032474

Manufactured in the United States of America
1 2 3 4 5 6 – JR – 11 10 09 08 07 06

TABLE OF CONTENTS

Introduction

Abigail Adams was the wife of one president and the mother of another. For these reasons alone, she earned a place in history.

But Abigail earned that place on her own too. She lived at a time when the United States was struggling to become a new country. She wrote letters that told what she saw happening. Her letters give us a peek at what life was like when the country was being born. They also show us a woman who had her own ideas about how to run that country.

This is her story.

ABIGAIL AND JOHN

Everyone in the Smith family always knew where to find Abigail. She was almost always in her father's library. Her father had lots of books. And wherever there were books, there was Abigail.

Abigail was born in November 1744. She grew up in the town of Weymouth, Massachusetts. She was still Abigail Smith then. And Massachusetts was still a colony of Great Britain.

Abigail was the kind of girl who wanted to learn *everything*. But she never spent a day in school. Girls in Abigail's time did not usually go to school. She and her two sisters learned at home. Only her brother went to school.

Her first teachers were her parents. They taught her to read and write. But her best teachers were books. Abigail's father encouraged her to read whatever she liked. Soon she was spending every spare minute curled up with one of her father's books.

Abigail Smith grew up in this house in Weymouth, Massachusetts.

Reading showed Abigail a whole world filled with ideas. She had ideas of her own too. And she always told people just what she thought. Abigail's mother wasn't so sure about this books-and-ideas business. She said that proper young ladies were supposed to be sweet and quiet. They weren't supposed to think too much or have too many opinions. But all her fussing couldn't change Abigail.

WHICH ONE ARE YOU?

People in Abigail's time liked to use the same first names over and over. Both her father and her brother were named William. Her grandmother, her mother, and her sister were all named Elizabeth. Abigail and her daughter had the same name too. Nicknames helped to keep things straight!

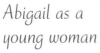
Abigail as a young woman

When Abigail was about seventeen, a young man began visiting the Smith home. He was a twenty-six-year-old lawyer named John Adams. Abigail learned that John liked books as much as she did. And he liked hearing what she thought about things.

Abigail began to think about John more and more. Sometimes they couldn't be together. So they wrote letters. She called him Dearest Friend. He called her Miss Adorable.

John Adams was Abigail's "dearest friend."

In the fall of 1764, Abigail and John were married. They settled into John's farmhouse in nearby Braintree. Their family grew quickly. The next summer, their first baby, a girl, was born. They named her Abigail, but they called her Nabby. Two years later, a son, John Quincy, was born.

Just as Abigail's family was growing, trouble was growing too. The trouble came from the British king and his lawmakers. They needed money. So they decided to get it from the colonies. And how were they going to get it? Taxes! The British taxed everything in the colonies from playing cards to tea.

King George III ruled over Great Britain from 1760 to 1820.

All those taxes didn't make the king very popular with the colonists. In nearby Boston, angry crowds shouted in the streets. Unfair, they said!

Abigail and John thought so too. John started writing articles for the newspaper. The people weren't allowed to vote for the king's lawmakers, he said. So they shouldn't have to pay the king's tax. Abigail agreed with every word.

Colonists rally against British taxes.

Boston, Massachusetts, was one of the most important cities in the colonies.

John's law work often took him to Boston. He began meeting with other men there. These men called themselves patriots. They were unhappy with the way Great Britain was treating the colonies. They liked what John had to say.

More and more, John was away from the farm. Abigail missed her "dearest friend" when he was gone. So in the spring of 1768, when she was twenty-three, she and John packed up books and clothes and babies. They were moving to Boston.

2 BOSTON

B*rrrumm! Brrrumm! Brrrumm!* Every
morning, Abigail awoke to the same
awful noise. British soldiers were marching
and drumming right under her window.

The soldiers were everywhere in Boston.
The king had sent them to keep order.
He hoped that all those red coats and
shiny weapons would scare the people
into behaving.

The king's plan didn't work out the way he expected. The people of Boston hated the sight of the soldiers. They called them names and threw snowballs at them. They pushed and pushed and waited for the soldiers to push back.

One cold night in March 1770, the pushing turned to bloodshed. Just two blocks from Abigail's front door, a mob of men and boys clashed with the soldiers. The frightened soldiers fired into the crowd. Abigail heard screams and shouts. She heard shots echoing through the chilly air. When it was over, five Americans lay bleeding to death in the snow.

Crispus Attucks (CENTER) was one of the colonists killed in the Boston Massacre on March 5, 1770.

As trouble kept growing in Boston, Abigail's family also kept growing. About three months after the deaths in the Boston Massacre, Abigail and John had another son. They named him Charles. (A daughter, Susanna, had died as a baby). Two years later another son, Thomas, was born.

By now, John was a leader in the struggle against Great Britain. He was a lawmaker in the Massachusetts government. With his clear, ringing voice, he spoke out for the rights he thought the colonists deserved.

THE BEST THING ABOUT BOSTON

Abigail was still the kind of person who wanted to learn everything. So she was very happy that Boston had four newspapers to read.

John's spirited words made him a leader among the patriots.

Abigail was proud of the work her husband was doing. But she knew there were dangers. The king might decide John was a traitor. Then John might be thrown in jail or even hanged. Still, Abigail promised that she would stand beside him no matter what might happen.

She and John often talked about politics long into the night. She always told him what she thought. John listened carefully to her opinions. He respected them. And he needed them. Abigail helped him make important decisions.

By 1773, Great Britain had gotten rid of most of the taxes. Only the tax on tea was left. But that one caused the most problems of all. The people decided they had had enough of the king's taxes—and his tea.

That December, three ships carrying tea dropped their anchors in Boston Harbor. A group of men dressed themselves up in blankets and feathers to look like Mohawk Indians. Then they sneaked aboard the tea ships and dumped all the tea into the harbor.

British tea filled the waters of Boston Harbor.

The events in Boston made King George III angry. He shut down the city's harbor.

When Abigail heard the news of the Boston Tea Party, she was delighted. The spirit of liberty was spreading like a fire, she wrote to a friend. But the king was not delighted at all. He quickly closed down the port in Boston. No ships—not even food ships—could go in or out.

The people of Boston might starve! That made leaders from all the colonies angry. They decided to hold a meeting in Philadelphia to decide what to do. The meeting was called the First Continental Congress. John would be one of the leaders at the meeting.

On August 10, 1774, twenty-nine-year-old Abigail kissed her "dearest friend" good-bye. Then she stood with the cheering crowds and watched John ride away. She knew that war with Great Britain was coming. "I cannot think of it without horror," she said.

J "REMEMBER THE LADIES"

Just as John had a job to do, so did Abigail. John would not earn much while he was in Congress. Abigail had to support the family. She had to go back to Braintree to run the farm.

Hired men did the daily farm chores. But it was Abigail who saw that everything was done properly. Abigail made sure that the fields were tended. She made sure the cows and chickens were fed. Abigail was in charge.

Nearly every evening, when her work was done, Abigail picked up her pen and wrote to John. When the cows in the field mooed from the heat, she told him. When rain watered the corn, she told him. And over and over again, she told him how much she missed him.

ABIGAIL THE TEACHER

Abigail couldn't spend all day being a farmer. It was her job to teach the children to read and write. As if that weren't enough, John had another idea. "It is time, my dear, for you to teach them French." So she did that too.

Then, on the night of April 18, 1775, British soldiers marched out of Boston. They headed toward the towns of Lexington and Concord. Armed Americans were already waiting for them there. The crack of gunfire told the news: the American Revolution had started.

The gunfire at Lexington and Concord is called "the shot heard 'round the world." It began the American Revolution.

Abigail had a war to write about. Frightened families were streaming out of Boston, she told John. Rumors of another attack sprouted like weeds. "You can hardly imagine how we live," she wrote.

One morning, in June 1775, she woke to the boom of cannons. With John Quincy, she climbed a nearby hill for a look. She wrote to John and told him what they had seen. She said that the hills of Charlestown just outside of Boston lay "in ashes."

Colonists in Boston watch the Battle of Bunker Hill near Charlestown, Massachusetts.

The First Continental Congress met in Carpenters' Hall in Philadelphia, Pennsylvania.

John depended on Abigail's reports. News was hard to come by in Philadelphia. After all, it was three hundred miles away from the war. Sometimes John shared Abigail's letters with other members of Congress. He boasted that he learned more from those letters than from "a whole committee of gentlemen."

Abigail also filled her letters with her own ideas. It was time to separate from Britain, she told John. It was time to make a new country, with new laws. But what should those laws be?

She had ideas on that too. There should be no more slavery in the new nation, she told him. People in the colonies were allowed to own slaves. But Abigail thought it wasn't fair to fight for freedom for themselves and then take it away from others.

This detail from a needlework picture shows an African American slave serving her mistress. Abigail believed that slavery was wrong.

Some colonial women proved they could do the same work as men. They could run a plantation or a large farm. Abigail felt women should have the same rights as men.

"And by the way," she wrote, "in the new code of laws . . . I desire you would remember the ladies." Women in Abigail's time could not vote or own property. Men had all the power. That was wrong, Abigail said. Women should have a voice in the new government. Or perhaps they'd make a revolution of their own!

John had always listened to Abigail's opinions. But this time he wrote, "I cannot but laugh." He made a joke of her idea! Abigail didn't think his joke was so funny.

Five men from the Continental Congress worked together on the Declaration of Independence. Abigail's husband, John (SECOND FROM RIGHT), was one of them.

Then, in July 1776, John wrote with the happiest news she could imagine. The men of Congress had decided to separate—once and for all—from Britain. They had signed the Declaration of Independence.

Abigail joined excited crowds when the Declaration was read in Boston. She described it all for John. People cheered, bells clanged, cannons thundered, and "every face appeared joyful," she said.

But the British wouldn't let go of the colonies just like that. The colonists would have to do more than declare their freedom. They would have to fight for it.

Fighting meant the country needed heroes. Well, Abigail told John, "If we mean to have heroes . . . we should have learned women." Girls must go to school along with boys, she said firmly. She didn't care if people laughed at her for saying it.

In November 1777, John came home to the farm. He was home, he said—to stay! Abigail had waited three years to hear those words. She hoped she and John would never be separated again.

4 ABIGAIL IN EUROPE

J ohn had been home only three weeks when news came. Congress was sending him away again! This time, it was sending him not three hundred miles away, but three *thousand*. He was going to France to ask its government for help with the war.

At once, Abigail's plans for life with John at home were gone. But she would not dream of asking him not to go. His country needed him.

This time, ten-year-old John Quincy would go too. The trip would be a good education, his parents decided. On a winter day in 1778, father and son left home for the long trip across the ocean.

Abigail was truly on her own. She had to make all the decisions. And she had to make more money. She asked John to send her fancy items made in Europe. Soon she was selling ribbons, lace, and dishes to Americans. Abigail had become a good merchant. The family's little pile of money began to grow.

This cupboard holds the kind of dishes Abigail may have sold to wealthy colonial women.

This statue in Quincy, Massachusetts, honors Abigail and her son John Quincy.

John and John Quincy came home in the summer of 1779. Abigail's family was together again. She couldn't have been happier! But the visit was short. Congress found more for John to do in Europe. He and John Quincy went back that fall. Nine-year-old Charles went too. The farmhouse was quieter than ever.

In September 1783, John signed a peace treaty with Britain. The patriots had won the war. The United States of America was free.

Still, John's work was not done. There were more matters to settle and more papers to sign. Except for short visits, he and Abigail had been separated for almost nine years. That was long enough! If John couldn't come home, Abigail would go to him.

So, at the age of thirty-nine, Abigail boarded a ship crossing the wide Atlantic Ocean. Eighteen-year-old Nabby went too. Charles had come home earlier. This time, he stayed home with Thomas.

In July 1784, Abigail and Nabby reached Europe. John and seventeen-year-old John Quincy greeted them with hugs and tears. They were a happy family again.

YES, MA'AM!

Abigail's voyage across the ocean didn't start out well at all. The ship was filthy, and the food was horrible. So she set the crew to work with mops and buckets. She gave the cook a few lessons too!

The family settled into a big house just outside Paris, France. For Abigail, Paris was a whole new world. She sent letter after letter back home. She wrote her niece that she hadn't seen much of the city yet. But, she said, "I have smelt it."

The people of Paris seemed to think of nothing but fun, she told a friend. At first, Abigail wasn't sure if she liked that. But she did get used to it. She even learned to enjoy the ballet—though at first, she thought the dancers were hopping about in their underwear!

In Paris, Abigail went to operas, such as this one.

One day, the family received big news. John was to be the very first person to represent the new United States to the British king. Abigail had to get used to living in a new city—London, England.

In London, John looked forward to meeting the king. Abigail wasn't so sure. She had to get all dressed up in a fancy gown with ruffles and ribbons. Then she stood around for hours with two hundred other people, waiting for the king to speak to her. She thought the whole thing was rather silly.

In London, the Adamses lived in a town house on Grosvenor Square (BELOW). More than 700,000 people lived in London in the late 1700s.

She did find things to like about London, though. She enjoyed talks on science. She learned how magnets worked and what electricity was. Learning about science "was like going into a beautiful country which I never saw before," she told her sister.

Still, Abigail missed her *own* country. She missed her two younger sons too. And back home, people were talking about a new set of laws—the U.S. Constitution. There would be a new government, and John wanted to be part of it.

Abigail and John agreed: it was time to go home.

5 A PRESIDENT'S WIFE

The Adamses had arranged to buy a new farmhouse in Braintree while they were away. But they wouldn't spend much time there. Four days after they arrived, the Constitution became law. An election was held to choose a leader for the United States. When the votes were counted in March 1789, George Washington was the president. And John was the vice president! It was time to pack again.

Abigail liked her pretty house in New York. (That city was the nation's capital at the time. Later, the capital moved to Philadelphia.) But she found that being a vice president's wife mostly meant going to parties. Balls, teas, and dull dinners took up most of her time. Once a week, she was expected to open her home to visitors. The whole evening was nothing but curtsies, polite talk, tea, and cake.

Abigail's home in New York had a view of the Hudson River.

Abigail did not think tea parties were very exciting.

Abigail never really liked these get-togethers. She was more interested in going to meetings of Congress. She'd take a lively speech over a tea party any day!

By 1796, it was time for a new election. Naturally, Abigail thought that John would make the best president. But she worried that she would not make a good First Lady. George Washington's wife, Martha, had always been quiet and proper. How could Abigail be quiet? Was she going to have to watch everything she said?

In early 1797, when the last vote of the election was counted, John had won. On March 4, in Philadelphia, he became the country's second president. But Abigail wasn't there to see it. She was sick at home. The children also missed the event. John Quincy was representing the country in Holland. His brother Thomas was with him. Nabby and Charles lived in New York with families of their own.

A few months later, Abigail joined John in Philadelphia. She read newspapers and met congressmen. As always, she told John just what she thought. And—as always— John needed her opinions. "I can do nothing without you," he told her.

Nabby (LEFT) and Charles did not go to Philadelphia when their father, John, was elected president. They had families of their own in New York.

Washington became the U.S. capital in 1800. Few people lived there yet when Abigail was First Lady.

In November 1800, the country had a new capital, Washington. And Abigail and John had a big new home. It would someday be known as the White House. Abigail called it "a castle of a house." And it was—at least on the outside.

Inside it was cold, damp, and smelly. The fresh plaster on the walls was still wet. The rooms were empty. And a whole staircase was missing. There was no place to hang laundry, either. So Abigail strung a clothesline in the grand East Room.

She and John had barely moved into their "castle" when it was time to leave. There had been another election. This time, John lost. In March 1801, Thomas Jefferson became president.

One more time, Abigail and John packed up books and clothes and papers. They moved back to the farm. John called himself Farmer John. Abigail rose before dawn to do chores.

Abigail was delighted to have her family around her again. Children, grandchildren, nieces, and nephews all came to the farm. Little ones chased Abigail's new puppy. They blew soap bubbles with John's pipe.

Abigail and John's home had lots of room for visiting relatives.

When her family was not there, Abigail wrote letters. As the years passed, age made her hands stiff. It was hard to hold a pen. Still, she wrote.

In October 1818, at the age of seventy-three, Abigail died. She left behind her "dearest friend," who would miss her very much. She also left behind nearly two thousand letters. Abigail had always said just what she thought. Now those letters would have to speak for her.

A PROUD MOTHER

Abigail loved all her children. But she was especially proud of John Quincy. He became a fine lawmaker, just like his father. In 1825, he became president of the United States.

TIMELINE

ABIGAIL ADAMS WAS BORN ON NOVEMBER 22, 1744.

In the year . . .

1764   Abigail married John Adams.   Age 19

1765   her daughter Nabby was born.

1767   Abigail's son John Quincy was born.

1768   she moved to Boston in the spring.
her daughter Susanna was born in December.

1770   Susanna died in February.
the Boston Massacre took place in March.
Abigail's son Charles was born in May.

1772   her son Thomas was born.

1773   the Boston Tea Party took place.

1774   John was elected to the Continental Congress.

1775   the Revolutionary War began.

1776   she asked John to "remember the ladies" in March.
the Declaration of Independence was signed in July.

1783   the American Revolution ended.

1784   she and Nabby joined John and John   Age 39
Quincy in France.

1785   Abigail moved to London.

1789   John became the first vice president of the United States.

1797   Abigail became the First Lady when John   Age 52
was elected the second president of the United States.

1800   she moved to the city of Washington.

1801   she returned home to Massachusetts.

1818   she died on October 28.   Age 73

"REMEMBER THE LADIES"

People saved the many letters that Abigail wrote during her life. After she died, the letters were published in a book. For the first time, others could read what Abigail had to say.

Women especially liked Abigail's ideas. They agreed that the government should "remember the ladies." In time, women really did have a revolution of their own. They demanded the right to vote. They protested and made speeches. "Remember the ladies!" became a familiar cry.

In 1920, lawmakers changed the U.S. Constitution. At last, women could vote. They had a voice in government. And Abigail's words had been a part of the fight.

Women announce a May 4, 1912, Votes for Women rally in New York City.

FURTHER READING

Byers, Helen. *Colors of France.* Minneapolis: First Avenue Editions, 2002. When Abigail went to see John in Paris, she visited a whole new world. Get a taste of France yourself with this book!

Ferris, Jeri Chase. *Remember the Ladies: A Story About Abigail Adams.* Minneapolis: Millbrook Press, 2001. Read even more about Abigail and her life.

Gherman, Beverly. *First Son and President: A Story About John Quincy Adams.* Minneapolis: Millbrook Press, 2006. Find out more about the life of Abigail and John's eldest son, who became the sixth U.S. president.

Ransom, Candice F. *Martha Washington.* Minneapolis: Carolrhoda Books, 2003. Abigail saw Martha Washington as an example of a proper First Lady. Learn more about Martha in this biography.

St. George, Judith. *John and Abigail Adams: An American Love Story.* New York: Holiday House, 2001. Find out more about John and Abigail's relationship.

Sutcliffe, Jane. *John Adams.* Minneapolis: Lerner Publishing Group, 2006. Learn more about Abigail's husband and dearest friend.

Sutcliffe, Jane. *Paul Revere.* Minneapolis: Lerner Publishing Group, 2002. Paul Revere was another important patriot. Read his story in this book!

Waters, Kate. *The Story of the White House.* New York: Scholastic, 1991. Abigail was the first First Lady to live in the White House. Explore the history of this building in this book.

WEBSITES

Abigail Smith Adams
http://www.whitehouse.gov/history/firstladies/aa2.html
This site presents Abigail's official White House biography.

Adams Family Papers
http://www.masshist.org/digitaladams/aea
Visit this online collection of writings by Abigail and John.

SELECT BIBLIOGRAPHY

Akers, Charles W. *Abigail Adams: An American Woman.* New York: HarperCollins Publishers, 1980.

Butterfield, L. H., M. Friedlander, and M. J. Kline, eds. *The Book of Abigail and John: Selected Letters of the Adams Family, 1762–1784.* Cambridge, MA: Harvard University Press, 1975.

Ching, Jacqueline. *Abigail Adams: A Revolutionary Woman.* New York: PowerPlus Books, 2002.

Gelles, Edith. *Abigail Adams: A Writing Life.* New York: Routledge, 2002.

Levin, Phyllis Lee. *Abigail Adams: A Biography.* New York: St. Martin's Press, 1987.

Shuffleton, Frank, ed. *The Letters of John and Abigail Adams.* New York: Penguin Books, 2004.

Withey, Lynne. *Dearest Friend: A Life of Abigail Adams.* New York: Simon & Schuster, 1981.

INDEX

Acknowledgments

For photographs and artwork: © The Granger Collection, NY, p. 4; Massachusetts Historical Society, p. 7; © North Wind Picture Archives, pp. 9, 17, 24, 32, 39; National Archives, pp. 10, 15, 28; Library of Congress, pp. 11 (LC-USZ62-7819), 12 (LC-USZ61-536), 13 (LC-USZ62-75184), 18 (LC-USZC4-523), 19 (LC-USZ62-45549), 23 (LC-DIG-ppmsca-05483), 27 (LC-USZ62-8452), 38 (LC-USZ62-95063), 41 (LC-USZC4-530), 45 (LC-USZ62-70383); Connecticut Historical Society, p. 26; From the collection of Henry Ford Museum and Greenfield Village (Neg. No. B45456. Acc. No. 30.471.27), p. 31; © Giraudon/Art Resource, NY, p. 34; © Stapleton Collection/ CORBIS, p. 35; Adams National Historical Park, pp. 40, 42. Front Cover: © Bettmann/CORBIS. Back Cover: Independence National Historical Park.

For quoted material: pp. 20, 21, 22, 24, 27, 28, 29, L. H. Butterfield, M. Friedlander, and M. J. Kline, ed., *The Book of Abigail and John: Selected Letters of the Adams Family, 1762-1784* (Cambridge, MA: Harvard University Press, 1975); p. 23, Ralph Waldo Emerson, "Concord Hymn," *National Center for Public Policy Research,* n.d., http://www.nationalcenter.org/ConcordHymn.html (March 22, 2006); pp. 25, 41, Lynne Withey, *Dearest Friend: A Life of Abigail Adams* (New York: Simon & Schuster, 1981); p. 27, Frank Shuffleton, ed., *The Letters of John and Abigail Adams* (New York: Penguin Books, 2004); p. 34, Edith Gelles, *Abigail Adams: A Writing Life* (New York: Routledge, 2002); p. 36, Phyllis Lee Levin, *Abigail Adams: A Biography* (New York: St. Martin's Press, 1987); p. 40, David McCullough, *John Adams* (New York: Simon & Schuster, 2001).